W9-AOC-976

To Susan Clark

LIBRA

A guide to living your best astrological life

STELLA ANDROMEDA

ILLUSTRATED BY EVI O. STUDIO

Hardie Grant

BOOKS

III.
Give Me More

Introduction

Inscribed on the forecourt of the ancient Greek temple of Apollo at Delphi are the words 'know thyself'. This is one of the 147 Delphic maxims, or rules to live by, attributed to Apollo himself, and was later extended by the philosopher Socrates to the sentence, 'The unexamined life is not worth living.'

People seek a variety of ways of knowing themselves, of coming to terms with life and trying to find ways to understand the challenges of human existence, often through therapy or belief systems like organised religion. These are ways in which we strive to understand the relationships we have with ourselves and others better, seeking out particular tools that enable us to do so.

As far as systems of understanding human nature and experience go, astrology has much to offer through its symbolic use of the constellations of the heavens, the depictions of the zodiac signs, the planets and their energetic effects. Many people find accessing this information and harnessing its potential a useful way of thinking about how to manage their lives more effectively.

What is astrology?

In simple terms, astrology is the study and interpretation of how the planets can influence us, and the world in which we live, through an understanding of their positions at a specific place in time. The practice of astrology relies on a combination of factual knowledge of the characteristics of these positions and their psychological interpretation.

Astrology is less of a belief system and more of a tool for living, from which ancient and established wisdom can be drawn. Any of us can learn to use astrology, not so much for divination or telling the future, but as a guidebook that provides greater insight and a more thoughtful way of approaching life. Timing is very much at the heart of astrology, and knowledge of planetary configurations and their relationship to each other at specific moments in time can assist in helping us with the timing of some of our life choices and decisions.

Knowing when major life shifts can occur – because of particular planetary configurations such as a Saturn return (see page 103) or Mercury retrograde (see page 104) – or what it means to have Venus in your seventh house (see pages 85 and 98), while recognising the specific characteristics of your sign, are all tools that you can use to your advantage. Knowledge is power, and astrology can be a very powerful supplement to approaching life's ups and downs and any relationships we form along the way.

The 12 signs of the zodiac

Each sign of the zodiac has a range of recognisable characteristics, shared by people born under that sign. This is your Sun sign, which you probably already know – and the usual starting point from which we each begin to explore our own astrological paths. Sun sign characteristics can be strongly exhibited in an individual's make-up; however, this is only part of the picture.

Usually, how we appear to others is tempered by the influence of other factors – and these are worth bearing in mind. Your ascendant sign is equally important, as is the positioning of your Moon. You can also look to your opposite sign to see what your Sun sign may need a little more of, to balance its characteristics.

After getting to know your Sun sign in the first part of this book, you might want to dive into the Give Me More section (see pages 74–105) to start to explore all the particulars of your birth chart. These will give you far greater insight into the myriad astrological influences that may play out in your life.

Sun signs

It takes 365 (and a quarter, to be precise) days for the Earth to orbit the Sun and in so doing, the Sun appears to us to spend a month travelling through each sign of the zodiac. Your Sun sign is therefore an indication of the sign that the Sun was travelling through at the time of your birth. Knowing what Sun signs you and your family, friends and lovers are provides you with just the beginning of the insights into character and personality that astrology can help you discover.

On the cusp

For those for whom a birthday falls close to the end of one Sun sign and the beginning of another, it's worth knowing what time you were born. There's no such thing, astrologically, as being 'on the cusp' – because the signs begin at a specific time on a specific date, although this can vary a little year on year. If you are not sure, you'll need to know your birth date, birth time and birth place to work out accurately to which Sun sign you belong. Once you have these, you can consult an astrologer or run your details through an online astrology site program (see page 108) to give you the most accurate birth chart possible.

Taurus

The bull

21 APRIL–20 MAY

Grounded, sensual and appreciative of bodily pleasures, Taurus is a fixed earth sign endowed by its ruling planet Venus with grace and a love of beauty, despite its depiction as a bull. Generally characterised by an easy and uncomplicated, if occasionally stubborn, approach to life, Taurus' opposite sign is watery Scorpio.

Aries

The ram

21 MARCH–20 APRIL

Astrologically the first sign of the zodiac, Aries appears alongside the vernal (or spring) equinox. A cardinal fire sign, depicted by the ram, it is the sign of beginnings and ruled by planet Mars, which represents a dynamic ability to meet challenges energetically and creatively. Its opposite sign is airy Libra.

Gemini

The twins

★

21 MAY–20 JUNE

A mutable air sign symbolised by
the twins, Gemini tends to see both
sides of an argument, its speedy
intellect influenced by its ruling
planet Mercury. Tending to fight
shy of commitment, this sign also
epitomises a certain youthfulness
of attitude. Its opposite sign is
fiery Sagittarius.

Cancer

The crab

★

21 JUNE–21 JULY

Depicted by the crab and the
tenacity of its claws, Cancer is a
cardinal water sign, emotional and
intuitive, its sensitivity protected
by its shell. Ruled by the maternal
Moon, the shell also represents the
security of home, to which Cancer
is committed. Its opposite sign is
earthy Capricorn.

Leo

The lion

✳

22 JULY–21 AUGUST

A fixed fire sign, ruled by the Sun, Leo loves to shine and is an idealist at heart, positive and generous to a fault. Depicted by the lion, Leo can roar with pride and be confident and uncompromising, with a great faith and trust in humanity. Its opposite sign is airy Aquarius.

Virgo

The virgin

✳

22 AUGUST–21 SEPTEMBER

Traditionally represented as a maiden or virgin, this mutable earth sign is observant, detail oriented and tends towards self-sufficiency. Ruled by Mercury, Virgos benefit from a sharp intellect that can be self-critical, while often being very health conscious. Its opposite sign is watery Pisces.

Scorpio

The scorpion

22 OCTOBER–21 NOVEMBER

Given to intense feelings, as
befits a fixed water sign, Scorpio
is depicted by the scorpion – linking
it to the rebirth that follows death –
and is ruled by both Pluto and Mars.
With a strong spirituality and deep
emotions, Scorpio needs security to
transform its strength. Its opposite
sign is earthy Taurus.

Libra

The scales

22 SEPTEMBER–21 OCTOBER

A cardinal air sign, ruled by Venus,
Libra is all about beauty, balance
(as depicted by the scales) and
harmony in its rather romanticised,
ideal world. With a strong aesthetic
sense, Libra can be both arty and
crafty, but also likes fairness and
can be very diplomatic. Its
opposite sign is fiery Aries.

Sagittarius

The archer

★

22 NOVEMBER–21 DECEMBER

Depicted by the archer, Sagittarius is a mutable fire sign that's all about travel and adventure, in body or mind, and is very direct in approach. Ruled by the benevolent Jupiter, Sagittarius is optimistic with lots of ideas; liking a free rein, but with a tendency to generalise. Its opposite sign is airy Gemini.

Capricorn

The goat

★

22 DECEMBER–20 JANUARY

Ruled by Saturn, Capricorn is a cardinal earth sign associated with hard work and depicted by the sure-footed and sometimes playful goat. Trustworthy and unafraid of commitment, Capricorn is often very self-sufficient and has the discipline for the freelance working life. Its opposite sign is the watery Cancer.

Pisces

The fish

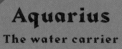

20 FEBRUARY–20 MARCH

Acutely responsive to its surroundings, Pisces is a mutable water sign depicted by two fish, swimming in opposite directions, sometimes confusing fantasy with reality. Ruled by Neptune, its world is fluid, imaginative and empathetic, often picking up on the moods of others. Its opposite sign is earthy Virgo.

Aquarius

The water carrier

21 JANUARY–19 FEBRUARY

Confusingly, given its depiction by the water carrier, Aquarius is a fixed air sign ruled by the unpredictable Uranus, sweeping away old ideas with innovative thinking. Tolerant, open-minded and all about humanity, its vision is social with a conscience. Its opposite sign is fiery Leo.

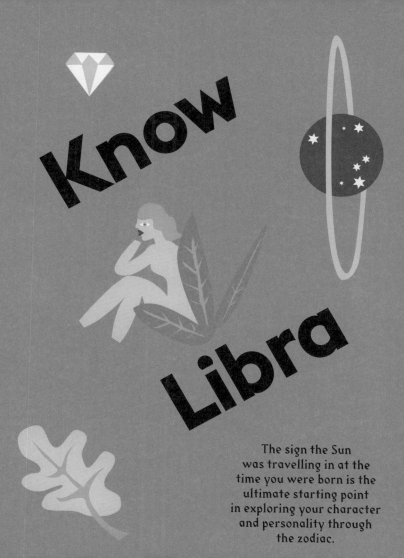

Know

Libra

The sign the Sun
was travelling in at the
time you were born is the
ultimate starting point
in exploring your character
and personality through
the zodiac.

Cardinal air sign,
depicted by the scales.

Ruled by Venus,
the planet associated with
the Roman goddess of beauty,
fertility, prosperity and love.

OPPOSITE SIGN

Aries

STATEMENT OF SELF

'I balance.'

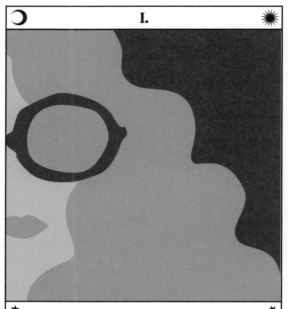

Lucky colour

Blue in its various shades, and pastel shades in particular. These cool, harmonious hues reflect a sophisticated flair – nothing brash or obvious or over-emphatic – that epitomises Libra. Wear these colours when you need a psychological boost, choosing accessories – shoes, gloves, socks or even underwear – if you don't want to commit head-to-toe.

Lucky day

Friday. The end of the working week for most of us, when hardworking Libra can look forward to some rest. Friday actually links the Old English goddess Frigg with her Roman counterpart, Venus, and we also see this in the French word for Friday, *Vendredi*.

Lucky gem

The opal, with its inner fire, is Libra's lucky gem, symbolising
hope, faithfulness and confidence and imparting greater
insight to its wearer. Opals were also said to have been
wept by Zeus as tears of joy after the defeat of the Titans;
and were once considered the jewel of kings.

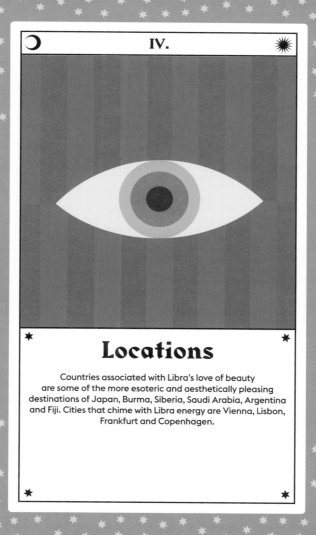

Locations

Countries associated with Libra's love of beauty
are some of the more esoteric and aesthetically pleasing
destinations of Japan, Burma, Siberia, Saudi Arabia, Argentina
and Fiji. Cities that chime with Libra energy are Vienna, Lisbon,
Frankfurt and Copenhagen.

Holidays

To relax, Libra needs beautiful surroundings, somewhere to chill and something to stimulate their airy intellect, making a cultural tour, with lots of beautiful art or architecture, music or dance, a serious contender, especially when it comes to city breaks. Music festivals, too, can appeal but there would need to be some serious glamping on offer, as Libra and muddy fields are seldom a good mix!

Flowers

The luxurious blooms of the blue Hydrangea appeal to the
Libra sense of style and beauty, while Cosmos daisy flowers
in their wide variety of blue shades also appeal.

Trees

The elegant almond tree, with its beautiful smelling blossom, is aligned to Libra, along with the tall, dark cypress and, for its peaceful connotations, the olive tree.

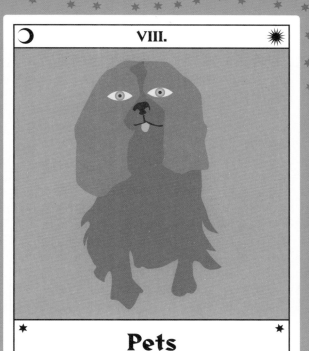

Pets

You might imagine something *scale-y* like a snake
for Libra, but their love of luxury and beauty, and desire
for reciprocal affection means a silky-haired
King Charles spaniel is more to their style.

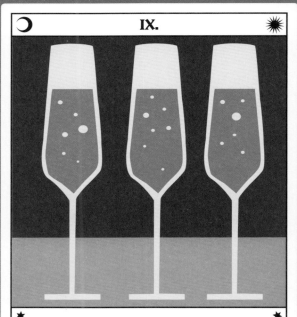

Parties

Parties thrown by Libra tend to be very stylish
and immaculately planned, with more of a Grecian toga
than a Mad Hatter's tea party vibe. There's a social
light-heartedness that befits an air sign and the potential
for lots of fizz: something like a Champagne cocktail using
a delicious *crème de pêche de vigne*, to give it a peachy
blush, might be on the menu.

Libra
characteristics

Key words for Libra are balance, harmony and diplomacy. Generally inclined to create peace, using silver-tongued words to soothe and placate, they are also good listeners and the least argumentative sign of the zodiac. That doesn't mean Libra doesn't enjoy debating the issue, in fact they relish it, weighing up the pros and cons of a situation, trying to balance both sides according to their astrological sign, the scales. There's a huge sense of fairness that drives them and an objectivity that allows Libra to see both sides. This ability to prioritise rational thought over feelings can often work in their favour, but can sometimes make them appear rather a reserved, cool customer. In fact, in extreme, this ability to see all sides can work against them, as others might distrust the Libra inclination to try to please all the people, all the time. That balancing act can sometimes look a little too much like sitting on the fence and Libra needs to remember that it's also important to say what they are actually thinking and feeling in order to communicate well, even at the risk of ruffling a few feathers.

That same sense of balance and harmony often shows up through an artistic appreciation or talent, whether that's an admiration for, or an ability to do, something beautiful, either through their own artistic effort or just in their home décor and the way they arrange something as simple as their beautifully laundered, linen tea towels. Libra's good taste is often demonstrated in the elegant way they dress. Even when their colours are bold, they'll be beautifully co-ordinated and there's an airy refinement which comes from attention to detail. What may be luxuries for others are necessities for Libra, whether that's freshly-ground, artisan-roasted beans for their coffee, the 600-thread count of their bed sheets or regular manicures and stylish haircuts.

Good-natured and good company, with an easy, sociable manner and smooth-talking repartee, Libra often has many acquaintances but fewer close friends. In fact, all that emotional balancing they do in their heads can create a sense of uncertainty, making it difficult for them to trust people and allow the intimacy that creates close bonds, and this uncertainty can sometimes be mistaken for self-reliance or airy indifference. But relationships are essential to Libra, they need them to balance themselves and thrive – so learning to manage these contradictions is important and, once a trusted bond has been made, that ambivalence can be overcome.

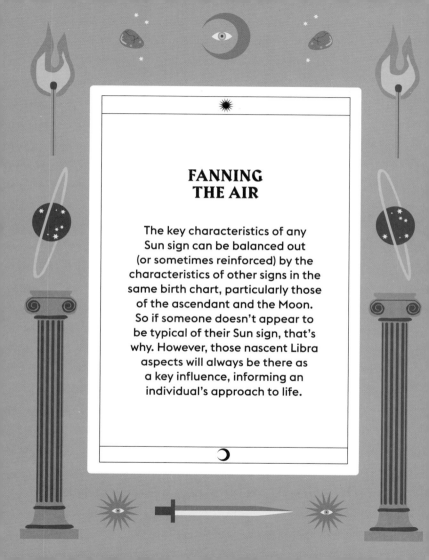

FANNING
THE AIR

The key characteristics of any
Sun sign can be balanced out
(or sometimes reinforced) by the
characteristics of other signs in the
same birth chart, particularly those
of the ascendant and the Moon.
So if someone doesn't appear to
be typical of their Sun sign, that's
why. However, those nascent Libra
aspects will always be there as
a key influence, informing an
individual's approach to life.

Physical Libra

Naturally graceful, there's a refinement about Libra that is enhanced by the way they present themselves, whether female or male. They tend not to rush in head first like their opposite sign, Aries, but take a more considered approach, and this is reflected in their body language and movements. Well-co-ordinated and usually with good posture, those physical activities that require good balance – like gymnastics or dancing – come naturally to Libra. Appearance matters, too: you won't find them neglecting to stay in good physical shape or holding on to mismatching socks, either. Libra tends to look smart even when they're in sweatpants.

Health

For Libra, the kidneys and lower, sacral area of the back can be susceptible to problems, and they may also be prone to sensitive skin and subject to occasional spotty break outs. Keeping the acid/alkaline balance of the body stable will help kidney function, ridding the body of toxins, and this will also help to support healthy skin. Lots of water to drink will keep fluid levels balanced, which also keeps the kidneys happy, while energy levels need to be balanced by adequate sleep and exercise, too. Exercise, in particular to keep the posture and the lower back strong, is also important.

Exercise

Regular, gentle exercise suits Libra and if it includes back-strengthening exercises, so much the better. Dance, or exercising to music, is a good choice, and the gracefulness of t'ai chi often appeals, along with Pilates for core strength and to support the back. If exercise is aesthetically pleasing in some way, Libra is more likely to persist.

How Libra communicates

As an air sign, Libra is usually extremely able to give voice to their ideas as verbal communication tends to come easily. A love of words and word play makes discussion and debate something on which Libra thrives, although that ability to constantly consider the pros and cons of any situation can make them rather long-winded, when sometimes just a straightforward yes or no would do. And while they are happy to give compliments when compliments are due, they are equally happy to explain exactly why, yes, your bum does look big in this, should you ask. What balances out their ability to talk is their ability to listen, making Libra a good and objective confidante. What Libra does have to remember, however, is that sometimes actions speak louder than words and communication also happens through the things we do as much as what we say.

Libra
careers

When it comes to work, like many other air signs Libra tends to excel in the world of ideas and intellect. This can be seen in an affinity with the spoken word, debating or negotiating, or in writing, all of which use words to good effect. Work needs to be both intellectually and socially stimulating and, being socially minded, Libra tends to prefer working in teams and with other people than alone. Balance and fairness are important too, which is why the law often attracts Libra, where they can also argue rationally and objectively, assessing both sides of an argument to ensure that good judgements are made.

The arts are another obvious source of career fulfilment for a sign that flourishes surrounded by lovely things. Not just the visual arts, but music and theatre and working in an environment where art is performed, exhibited or treasured. At an art gallery or museum, in art sales or as an agent, dealing with people to promote art or curating exhibitions: all might appeal to Libra. This interest in creating beautiful things can extend to graphic design or fashion, or experiences that include performance arts, and dance in particular.

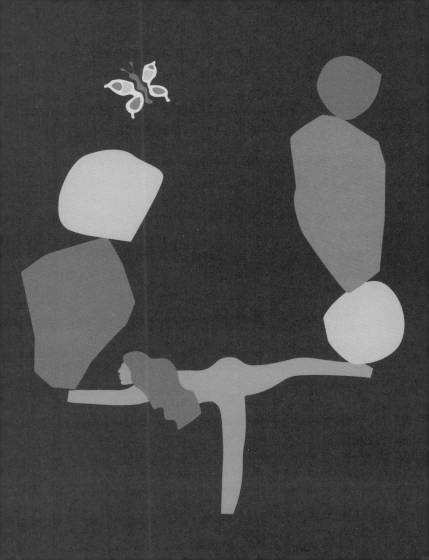

How
Libra
chimes

From lovers to friends, when it comes to other signs, how does Libra get along? Knowledge of other signs and how they interact can be helpful when negotiating relationships, revealed through an understanding of Sun sign characteristics that might chime or chafe. Understanding these through an astrological framework can be really helpful as it can depersonalise potential frictions, taking the sting out of what appears to be in opposition.

Harmonising relationships comes easily to Libra, the sign of balance, but how they chime is partly dependent on what other planetary influences are at play in their personal birth chart, toning down or enhancing aspects of their Sun sign characteristics, especially those that can sometimes clash with other signs.

The Libra woman

The Libra woman isn't always easy to read, because she is constantly trying to balance intellect and emotion, which can make her appear to blow hot and cold, making romantic gestures and then questioning them. With a tendency to take great care over her appearance, the Libra woman strives for perfection from her eyebrows to her toes and expects to be admired and complimented for it.

NOTABLE LIBRA WOMEN

Kim Kardashian and Gwyneth Paltrow may be the opposite ends of the Libra spectrum when it comes to looks, but their attention to glamorous detail at the nail bar or on the yoga mat is the same. Even on the tennis court Serena Williams exudes style, while Bella Hadid always embodies the current 'look' in fashion, and Susan Sarandon continues to demonstrate class on the red carpet.

The Libra man

There's a definite look to a Libra man: he's all about quality not quantity. He may not wear socks, but his shoes will be Italian, his shirts linen and sweaters cashmere. He's also a man who thrives on relationships, often more than one at a time until he decides where his heart truly rests, and charming enough to get away with it.

NOTABLE LIBRA MEN

Zac Efron, Will Smith and Dan Stevens are all suave Libras both on and off screen, a trait also embodied by one of the original James Bonds, Roger Moore, and that silver-tongued talent spotter Simon Cowell. The Libra talent is also there in the charisma of performers like John Lennon, Ray Charles and Sting.

Who love
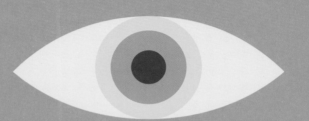

whom?

Libra & Aries

The physical connection between air and fire can easily ignite, but although there's often an initial attraction to Aries' passion, there can occasionally be friction because of Libra's more reserved style.

Libra & Taurus

There's a real connection here in their mutual love of art and music, and, both being ruled by Venus, there's an appreciation of life's luxuries. And although there's a good sexual connection too, Libra can sometimes find Taurus' earthy approach a little heavy.

Libra & Gemini

There's a lightness in this happy combination, as both air signs take pleasure in flirting and while there's probably a lot more talk than action, thanks to their mutual inclination toward indecision, they will eventually charm each other into bed.

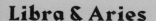

Libra &
Cancer

Cancer's watery need for
emotional responsiveness may
be a challenge for airy Libra,
whose commitment to the home
tends to be fairly superficial
compared to the crab's,
requiring thoughtfulness and
communication on both sides
to avoid misunderstanding.

Libra & Leo

Libra is tactful enough to
manage Leo's hot-blooded ego,
and their mutual playfulness
and love of socialising creates
an instantaneous initial bond
on which to build. However, that
inner reserve is no match for the
lion's sensual fire.

Libra & Virgo

There can be too much light-
heartedness in Libra's airy approach
for the rather serious, earthy Virgo.
Although the initial attraction of
opposites can work well, it just needs
some give and take on both sides to
get beyond their basic differences.

Libra &
Scorpio

Love between these two can
be pretty heady at first, but
that sting in the tail might be
too much for diplomatic Libra,
and their rather airy, flirtatious
approach to sex might not find
a balance in sensual Scorpio's
intense attitude.

Libra & Libra

While they easily recognise
each other, there's not much
to ground them and it can feel
a bit as if they are playing at
love, rather than really feeling
it. When it comes to balance,
they may need more from their
partner to get beyond that
first attraction.

Libra &
Sagittarius

Romance features strongly
when these two pair up, with
Sagittarius finding Libra's
intellect and charm intriguing
and difficult to resist. In turn,
the fire sign's outgoing and
adventurous attitude appeals,
freeing up Libra's reserve.

Libra &
Aquarius

These two air signs have much in
common but it's the experimental side
of Aquarius that initially piques Libra's
interest, waking them up to new
ideas and experiences. Harmonious
friendship is a strong connection here,
too, underpinning any relationship.

Libra & Pisces

A strong romantic connection gets
them off to a good start, but Pisces'
sentimental side can sometimes irritate
the more outgoing Libra who needs
to socialise, and isn't always able to
reassure Pisces that they really care
enough as they head for the door.

Libra &
Capricorn

Initially tricky, there can be
an immediate clash because
Capricorn isn't always able
to see beyond Libra's more
frivolous exterior, but this can
sometimes be overcome by
a strong physical connection,
thanks to the realistic nature
of the goat.

Libra love-o-meter

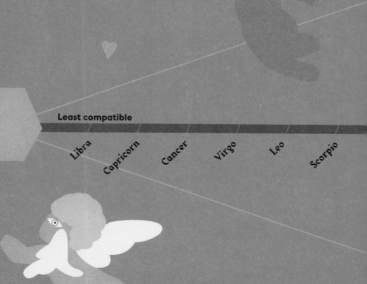

Least compatible

Libra · Capricorn · Cancer · Virgo · Leo · Scorpio

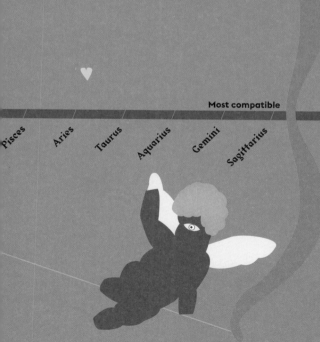

Most compatible

Pisces Aries Taurus Aquarius Gemini Sagittarius

The Libra

II.

Deep Dive

In this section, dive deeper
into the ways in which your
Sun sign might be driving
you or holding you back, and
start to think about how you
might use this knowledge
to inform your path.

The
Libra
home

The Libra home is generally uncluttered, with items of interest or beauty – from the quality of their bookshelves to a specific painting on the wall – carefully displayed and ready to be admired. Whether it's from Ikea, bespoke or from an architectural salvage company, furniture will be carefully chosen for its style as much as comfort. Libra would prefer to have one beautiful thing, such as a woven rug or a hand-glazed jug, than multiple possessions.

Libra may also express their desire for a serene environment in their choice of colours, possibly harmonising different shades of blue. Interior design, making their home lovely – whether it's a studio flat or a mansion – is source of real pleasure to Libra, not so much because they cherish their home for its own sake, but as a statement of personal style. In a way, Libra's home not only showcases their inner desire for balance but can also express some of that inner conflict, making it a good idea to team up with someone who is less about the ideas, and more about the practical detail, in order to get things done.

TOP TIPS FOR
LIBRA SELF-CARE

★ Stop ruminating and shift
   perspective with a walk in
   the park or even just around
   the block.

★ Balance socialising with a solo
   trip to an art gallery to replenish
   those batteries.

★ Keep a notebook to keep track
   of those ideas and plans.

Self-care

You'd think self-care would come easily to a sign invested in necessities that the rest of us might consider luxuries, like saunas and massage, but living in their head as much as Libra does sometimes means their body gets disregarded. Ignoring the mind/body link can mean that Libra doesn't always see the value of taking a walk to clear their head, particularly when indecision sets in. Without paying attention to the necessity to address this, it's all too possible for indecisive thoughts to move into anxiety and depression. Libra may think that restoring internal balance is done purely through the mind, but physical exercise is hugely beneficial in this process too. Once Libra has worked this out, then balancing their mental health through their physical health makes more sense and gets a whole lot easier. Some form of daily exercise is well worth making a habit in order to balance an excess of head work in which Libra can sometimes get stuck.

With a love of art and music, there's also all sorts of ways to refresh the Libra spirit, and this is equally important. Sometimes they just have to press pause, and take some time out. That way, Libra can restore both their internal and external balance, which will also improve sleep and energy levels, supporting busy lives.

WHAT TO KEEP IN THE LIBRA PANTRY

★ Pearled spelt as an alternative grain that adds balance to a dish.

★ Black truffle pesto to create glamour in a simple tagliatelle.

★ Minimum 75% cacao solids, artisanal chocolate for cooking (and nibbling).

Food
and
cooking

When Libra dons an apron in the kitchen, it's not so much about the food, but its quality and presentation. Enjoyment of food is one thing, but there's nothing slapdash about how Libra likes to prepare a meal. Part of the pleasure of creating a feast for family or friends is in the detailed preparation and, as for other air signs, the thinking and planning of a meal is often part of its attraction. The only drawback for Libra is deciding what to actually cook! But even if it's just a boiled egg, it's likely the egg will be fresh, free range and cooked to perfection, while the toast fingers are unlikely to be made from a three-day old, plastic-wrapped, sliced white loaf. If they've not baked it themselves, it's probably an artisanal, stone-ground wholemeal or sourdough loaf. Anyone receiving a dinner invite from Libra can anticipate something both tasty and well presented, from the place settings to the plating up of the food.

TOP TIPS FOR LIBRA'S MONEY

* Guard against spending too frivolously; bills still need to be paid.

* Remember to keep something aside for a 'rainy day' – that luxury can wait.

* Once the pros and cons of any investment are understood, act: don't lose out through indecision.

How Libra handles money

Money is only a motivating factor for Libra in as much as it enables them to buy the absolute best they can afford. However, while they definitely want to create a lovely home and acquire possessions, they don't really enjoy the graft sometimes necessary to achieve this.

Not natural risk takers, Libra tends to weigh up all the pros and cons of any deal. Staying in the black is their preferred option, while going into the red is usually a carefully calculated short-term means to an end, rather than an extravagant gesture. This sort of considered approach can make Libra very canny when it comes to money, while any investment in something like works of art will be done because they genuinely appreciate the art, not because the art will appreciate (but it probably will as they also have a good eye for both art and its market).

How Libra handles the boss

Skilled in the art of tact, diplomacy and smooth talking, Libra finds it possible to run rings around an unsuspecting boss, but because they are genuinely committed to the notion of fairness, they seldom take advantage of this. Rather, the Libra aim is to make working life harmonious for everyone, so they will often be the peacemakers in the office, too. This makes Libra a popular employee and happy to work in a team, although frequently they are also the team leader on whom the boss comes to rely.

Libra can get troublesome at work, however, if they feel they – or a colleague – are not being treated fairly. Woe betide any boss who doesn't stick to gender, race or class equality in the workplace, for example, as Libra will be the first to point this out – tactfully, maybe, but not without due emphasis and with all the relevant legislation to hand. Negotiation skills are often in evidence here, which means Libra volunteers or is informally elected to speak on behalf of others, as their ability to handle the boss is recognised by their team mates, too.

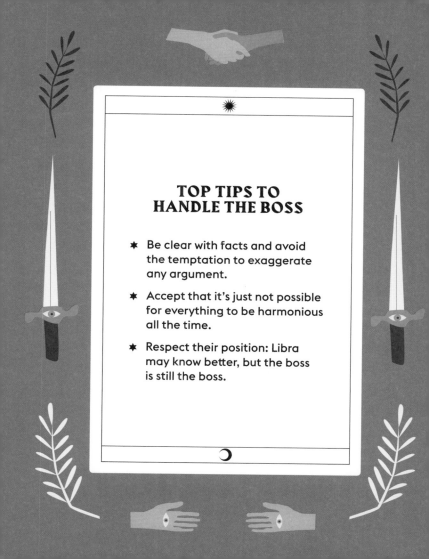

TOP TIPS TO HANDLE THE BOSS

★ Be clear with facts and avoid the temptation to exaggerate any argument.

★ Accept that it's just not possible for everything to be harmonious all the time.

★ Respect their position: Libra may know better, but the boss is still the boss.

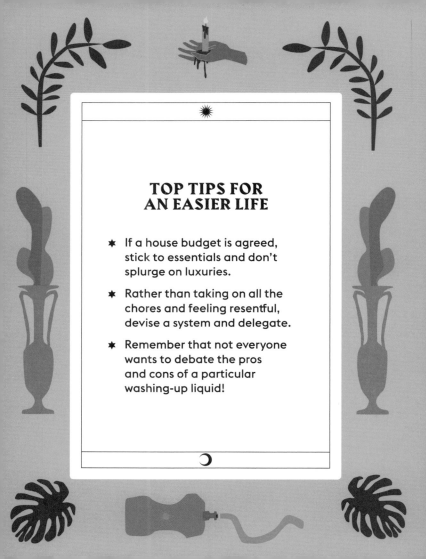

TOP TIPS FOR
AN EASIER LIFE

★ If a house budget is agreed,
stick to essentials and don't
splurge on luxuries.

★ Rather than taking on all the
chores and feeling resentful,
devise a system and delegate.

★ Remember that not everyone
wants to debate the pros
and cons of a particular
washing-up liquid!

What is Libra
like to live with?

Living with Libra is, in theory, pretty easy, but the demand for a harmonious life can sometimes be very much on their terms. This trait may not be immediately obvious, because they can be so charming and are willing to discuss and debate issues, but often housemates find themselves persuaded into agreeing just to end the conversation!

Home isn't as much of a priority as it is to some of the other signs, but how it looks matters deeply to Libra and even if they don't have a sentimental attachment to things, they will still want the best that they can afford. Their personal taste may make them quite fussy about where housemates leave their things, and cluttering up beautifully arranged *objets d'art* won't not go down well with Libra who can find sharing space tricky because of this.

Generally well disposed to being clean and tidy, Libra will go a long way to avoid an argument about whose turn it is to do the washing up or hoover the stairs, sometimes just by doing it themselves. In spite of a tendency to shy away from conflict, if they feel they are being treated unfairly, then Libra hackles can rise and squabbles can occur – but it does take quite a lot to provoke outright confrontation.

How to handle a break-up

Libra is the sign of partnerships and can be very invested in a relationship for its own sake. They may hang on until it is well past its sell-by date because they are often as committed to the relationship itself as they are to the person concerned. They also hate to hurt anyone's feelings.

While break-ups are tough for everyone, Libra always wants to try to understand *why* it has happened, and the reasons for it. Like other air signs that try to think their way through a problem, Libra often tries to work out how they, or their partner, are feeling, but it's just not always possible. This can be a hard lesson for Libra, but something that can actually be learnt from a break-up, irrespective of who wants to break up from whom.

TOP TIPS FOR
AN EASIER BREAK-UP

* After a break-up, don't expect an ex to want to discuss why ...

* ... and delete their number from the phone to resist calling.

* Accept that a break-up can open another door, in time.

How Libra wants to be loved

Ruled by Venus, the goddess of love, Libra is all about the romance of love. They love romancing and being romanced, and they feel much more balanced generally when they are in love or in a loving relationship, and a little out of sorts when not. This can sometimes mean that Libra likes to be in love for love's sake, delighting in the romance while sometimes losing sight of the relationship itself (or its more tedious aspects like putting the rubbish out). And being an air sign, Libra likes nothing better than talking about love, the subject of their love, and the ways in which they love their love and their love loves them. Get the picture? The downside of this is that when they really fall in love, it's not always easy for a partner to tell how committed they are and Libra needs to remember that it's not so much what you say, but what you do, that counts.

Libra is a sign that loves to be admired, and even worshipped, as much from a distance as close up, partly because in spite of all their apparent social ease, they are not always the most self-confident of signs. Constant reassurance suggests they're needy, but it's not so much that, it's just that the endless internal weighing up of the situation can undermine their self-worth. Even while Libra tends to have good instincts generally, they are sometimes afraid to trust them. Talking about the relationship with their partner is sometimes done in an effort to make it all seem more real, grounded and trustworthy.

As something of an idealist, Libra also tends to project their ideals onto their partner, which can make it easy for them to be disappointed; and to keep the reality of their relationship at arm's length. Deep down however, they are as vulnerable as any to the pursuit of real love. Don't be fooled by that Libra charm and gloss; their reserve creates a bit of a 'look but don't touch' coolness, but when they find someone who will allow them to let their guard down, this sign makes a great lover.

TOP TIPS FOR LOVING LIBRA

★ Talk to them. Strong and silent isn't enough – tell them how you feel.

★ Romance in all its forms is an important factor in keeping a relationship strong.

★ Appreciate that appearance will often matter – theirs and yours.

Libra's sex life

Sex for Libra is seldom focused just on the body but also needs a strong mental connection, so much so that even talking about sex can be very arousing. Erotic pleasure is often quite creative, with Libra paying a lot of attention to seduction and foreplay. The skin is very sensitive and being stroked and massaged can easily turn Libra on, especially the back, the lower back and the buttocks, all of which are markedly erogenous areas of their body. As much as being pleased, Libra gains a great deal of pleasure from pleasing their partner, and watching their partner's sexual pleasure. Mutual enjoyment definitely makes lovemaking more erotic for Libra, which in turn makes them unselfish lovers.

Libra needs to feel they're appreciated, though, and they need to hear encouraging words, to which they happily respond. Libra can often be quite reserved and discriminating, in spite of appearing so sexually confident and up front about what they want. They need a balance, but there's a subtle line and anything too crude or aggressive can sometimes be a turn off. Romance and verbal exchange fire up sexual attraction for Libra, while compliments and flattery in the bedroom helps fuel this further.

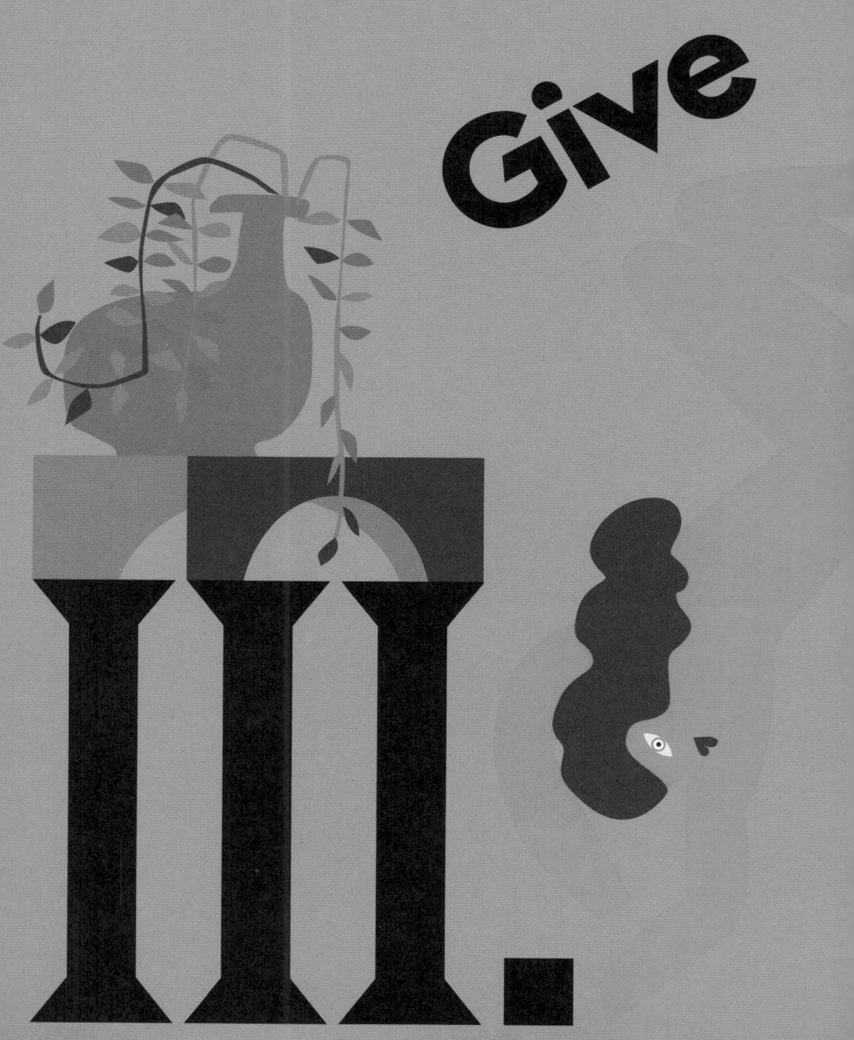
Give

Me

More

Your Sun sign never shows you the whole picture. In this section, learn how to read the nuances of your birth chart and discover a whole new level of astrological insight.

Your
birth
chart

Your birth chart is a snapshot of a particular moment, in a particular place, at the precise moment of your birth and is therefore completely individual to you. It's like a blueprint, a map, a statement of occurrence, spelling out possible traits and influences – but it isn't your destiny. It is just a symbolic tool to which you can refer, based on the position of the planets at the time of your birth. If you can't get to an astrologer, these days anyone can get their birth chart prepared in minutes online (see page 108 for a list of websites and apps that will do it for you). Even if you don't know your exact time of birth, just knowing the date and place of birth can create the beginnings of a useful template.

Remember, nothing is intrinsically good or bad in astrology and there is no explicit timing or forecasting: it's more a question of influences and how these might play out positively or negatively. And if we have some insight, and some tools with which to approach, see or interpret our circumstances and surroundings, this gives us something to work with.

When you are reading your birth chart, it's useful to first understand all the tools of astrology available to you; not only the astrological signs and what they represent, but also the 10 planets referred to in astrology and their individual characteristics, along with the 12 houses and what they mean. Individually, these tools of astrology are of passing interest, but when you start to see how they might sit in juxtaposition to each other, then the bigger picture becomes more accessible and we begin to gain insights that can be useful to us.

Broadly speaking, each of the planets suggests a different type of energy, the astrological signs propose the various ways in which that energy might be expressed, while the houses represent areas of experience in which this expression might operate.

Next to bring into the picture are the positions of the signs at four key points: the ascendant, or rising sign, and its opposite, the descendant; and the midheaven and its opposite, the IC, not to mention the different aspects created by congregations of signs and planets.

It is now possible to see how subtle the reading of a birth chart might be and how it is infinite in its variety, and highly specific to an individual. With this information, and a working understanding of the symbolic meaning and influences of the signs, planets and houses of your unique astrological profile, you can begin to use these tools to help with decision-making and other aspects of life.

Reading your chart

If you have your birth chart prepared, either by hand or via an online program, you will see a circle divided into 12 segments, with information clustered at various points indicating the position of each zodiac sign, in which segment it appears and at what degree. Irrespective of the features that are relevant to the individual, each chart follows the same pattern when it comes to interpretation.

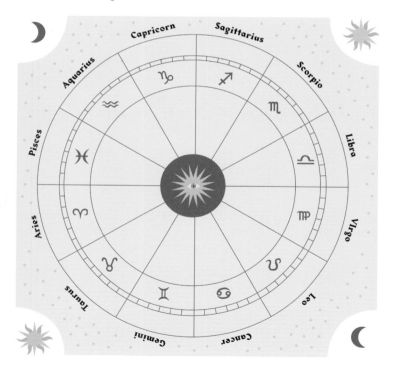

Given the time of birth, the place of birth and the position of the planets at that moment, the birth chart, sometimes called a natal horoscope, is drawn up.

If you consider the chart as a clock face, the first house (see pages 95–99 for the astrological houses) begins at the 9, and it is from this point that, travelling anti-clockwise the chart is read from the first house, through the 12 segments of the chart to the twelfth.

The beginning point, the 9, is also the point at which the Sun rises on your life, giving you your ascendant, or rising sign, and opposite to this, at the 3 of the clock face, is your descendant sign. The midheaven point of your chart, the MC, is at 12, and its opposite, the IC, at 6 (see pages 101–102).

Understanding the significance of the characteristics of the astrological signs and the planets, their particular energies, their placements and their aspects to each other can be helpful in understanding ourselves and our relationships with others. In day-to-day life, too, the changing configuration of planets and their effects are much more easily understood with a basic knowledge of astrology, as are the recurring patterns that can sometimes strengthen and sometimes delay opportunities and possibilities. Working with, rather than against, these trends can make life more manageable and, in the last resort, more successful.

The Moon effect

If your Sun sign represents your consciousness, your life force and your individual will, then the Moon represents that side of your personality that you tend to keep rather secret or hidden. This is the realm of instinct, intuition, creativity and the unconscious, which can take you places emotionally that are sometimes hard to understand. This is what brings great subtlety and nuance to a person, way beyond just their Sun sign. So you may have your Sun in Libra, and all that means, but this might be countered by a free-spirited and energetic Moon in Aries; or you may have your Sun in open-hearted Leo, but a Moon in Aquarius with all its rebellious, emotional detachment.

Phases of the Moon

The Moon orbits the Earth, taking roughly 28 days to do so. How much of the Moon we see is determined by how much of the Sun's light it reflects, giving us the impression that it waxes, or grows, and wanes. When the Moon is new, to us, only a sliver of it is illuminated. As it waxes, it reflects more light and moves from a crescent, to a waxing crescent to a first quarter; then it moves to a waxing gibbous Moon, to a full Moon. Then the Moon begins to wane through a waning gibbous, to a last quarter, and then the cycle begins again. All of this occurs over four weeks. When we have two full Moons in any one calendar month, the second is called a blue Moon.

Each month the Moon also moves through an astrological sign, as we know from our personal birth charts. This, too, will yield information – a Moon in Scorpio can have a very different effect to one in Capricorn – and depending on our personal charts, this can have a shifting influence each month. For example, if the Moon in your birth chart is in Virgo, then when the actual Moon moves into Virgo, this will have an additional influence. Read the characteristics of the signs for further information (see pages 12–17).

The Moon's cycle has an energetic effect, which we can see quite easily on the ocean tides. Astrologically, because the Moon is both a fertility symbol and attuned to our deeper psychological side, we can use this to focus more profoundly and creatively on aspects of life that are important to us.

Eclipses

Generally speaking, an eclipse covers up and prevents light being shed on a situation. Astrologically speaking, this will depend on where the Sun or Moon is positioned in relation to other planets at the time of an eclipse. So if a solar eclipse is in Gemini, there will be a Geminian influence or an influence on Geminis.

Hiding, or shedding, light on an area of our lives is an invitation to pay attention to it. Eclipses are generally about beginnings or endings, which is why our ancestors saw them as portents, important signs to be taken notice of. As it is possible to know when an eclipse is forthcoming, these are charted astronomically; consequently, their astrological significance can be assessed and acted upon ahead of time.

The 10 planets

For the purpose of astrology (but not for astronomy, because the Sun is really a star) we talk about 10 planets, and each astrological sign has a ruling planet, with Mercury, Venus and Mars each being assigned two. The characteristics of each planet describe those influences that can affect signs, all of which information feeds into the interpretation of a birth chart.

The Moon

This sign is an opposing principle to the Sun, forming a pair, and it represents the feminine, symbolising containment and receptivity, how we react most instinctively and with feeling.

Rules the sign of Cancer.

The Sun

The Sun represents the masculine, and is seen as the energy that sparks life, which suggests a paternal energy in our birth chart. It also symbolises our self or essential being, and our purpose.

Rules the sign of Leo.

Mercury

Mercury is the planet of communication and symbolises our urge to make sense of, understand and communicate our thoughts through words.

Rules the signs of Gemini and Virgo.

Venus

The planet of love is all about attraction, connection and pleasure and in a female chart it symbolises her style of femininity, while in a male chart it represents his ideal partner.

Rules the signs of Taurus and Libra.

Mars

This planet symbolises pure energy (Mars was, after all, the god of War) but it also tells you in which areas you're most likely to be assertive, aggressive or to take risks.

Rules the signs of Aries and Scorpio.

Saturn

Saturn is sometimes called the wise teacher or taskmaster of astrology, symbolising lessons learnt and limitations, showing us the value of determination, tenacity and resilience.

Rules the sign of Capricorn.

Jupiter

The planet Jupiter is the largest in our solar system and symbolises bounty and benevolence, all that is expansive and jovial. Like the sign it rules, it's also about moving away from the home on journeys and exploration.

Rules the sign of Sagittarius.

Uranus

This planet symbolises the unexpected, new ideas and innovation, and the urge to tear down the old and usher in the new. The downside can mark an inability to fit in and consequently the feeling of being an outsider.

Rules the sign of Aquarius.

Pluto

Aligned to Hades (*Pluto* in Latin), the god of the underworld or death, the planet exerts a powerful force that lies below the surface and which, in its most negative form, can represent obsessions and compulsive behaviour.

Rules the sign of Scorpio.

Neptune

Linked to the sea, this is about what lies beneath, underwater and too deep to be seen clearly. Sensitive, intuitive and artistic, it also symbolises the capacity to love unconditionally, to forgive and forget.

Rules the sign of Pisces.

The four elements

Further divisions of the 12 astrological signs into the four elements of earth, fire, air and water yield other characteristics. This comes from ancient Greek medicine, where the body was considered to be made up of four bodily fluids or 'humours'. These four humours – blood, yellow bile, black bile and phlegm – corresponded to the four temperaments of sanguine, choleric, melancholic and phlegmatic, to the four seasons of the year, spring, summer, autumn, winter, and the four elements of air, fire, earth and water.

Related to astrology, these symbolic qualities cast further light on characteristics of the different signs. Carl Jung also used them in his psychology, and we still refer to people as earthy, fiery, airy or wet in their approach to life, while sometimes describing people as 'being in their element'. In astrology, those Sun signs that share the same element are said to have an affinity, or an understanding, with each other.

Like all aspects of astrology, there is always a positive and a negative, and a knowledge of any 'shadow side' can be helpful in terms of self-knowledge and what we may need to enhance or balance out, particularly in our dealings with others.

Air

GEMINI ✳ LIBRA ✳ AQUARIUS

The realm of ideas is where these air signs excel. Perceptive and visionary and able to see the big picture, there is a very reflective quality to air signs that helps to vent situations. Too much air, however, can dissipate intentions, so Gemini might be indecisive, Libra has a tendency to sit on the fence, while Aquarius can be very disengaged.

Fire

ARIES ✳ LEO ✳ SAGITTARIUS

There is a warmth and energy to these signs, a positive approach, spontaneity and enthusiasm that can be inspiring and very motivational to others. The downside is that Aries has a tendency to rush in headfirst, Leo can have a need for attention and Sagittarius can tend to talk it up but not deliver.

Earth

TAURUS ✴ VIRGO ✴ CAPRICORN

Characteristically, these signs enjoy sensual pleasure, enjoying food and other physical pleasures, and they like to feel grounded, preferring to base their ideas in facts. The downside is that Taureans can be stubborn, Virgos can be pernickety and Capricorns can veer towards a dogged conservatism.

Water

CANCER ✴ SCORPIO ✴ PISCES

Water signs are very responsive, like the tide ebbing and flowing, and can be very perceptive and intuitive, sometimes uncannily so because of their ability to feel. The downside is – watery enough – a tendency to feel swamped, and then Cancer can be both tenacious and self-protective, Pisces chameleon-like in their attention and Scorpio unpredictable and intense.

Cardinal, fixed and mutable signs

In addition to the 12 signs being divided into four elements, they can also be grouped into three different ways in which their energies may act or react, giving further depth to each sign's particular characteristics.

Cardinal

ARIES ✳ CANCER ✳ LIBRA ✳ CAPRICORN

These are action planets, with an energy that takes the initiative and gets things started. Aries has the vision, Cancer the feelings, Libra the contacts and Capricorn the strategy.

Fixed

TAURUS ✴ LEO ✴ SCORPIO ✴ AQUARIUS

Slower but more determined, these signs work to progress and maintain those initiatives that the cardinal signs have fired up. Taurus offers physical comfort, Leo loyalty, Scorpio emotional support and Aquarius sound advice. You can count on fixed signs, but they tend to resist change.

Mutable

GEMINI ✴ VIRGO ✴ SAGITTARIUS ✴ PISCES

Adaptable and responsive to new ideas, places and people, mutable signs have a unique ability to adjust to their surroundings. Gemini is mentally agile, Virgo is practical and versatile, Sagittarius visualises possibilities and Pisces is responsive to change.

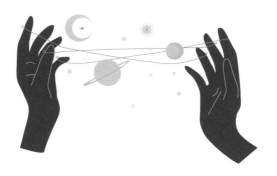

The 12 houses

The birth chart is divided into 12 houses, which represent separate areas and functions of your life. When you are told you have something in a specific house – for example, Libra (balance) in the fifth house (creativity and sex) – it creates a way of interpreting the influences that can arise and are particular to how you might approach an aspect of your life.

Each house relates to a Sun sign, and in this way each is represented by some of the characteristics of that sign, which is said to be its natural ruler.

Three of these houses are considered to be mystical, relating to our interior, psychic world: the fourth (home), eighth (death and regeneration) and twelfth (secrets).

1st House

THE SELF

RULED BY ARIES

This house symbolises the self: you, who you are and how you
represent yourself, your likes, dislikes and approach to life. It also
represents how you see yourself and what you want in life.

2nd House

POSSESSIONS

RULED BY TAURUS

The second house symbolises
your possessions, what you own,
including money; how you earn
or acquire your income; and your
material security and the physical
things you take with you as you
move through life.

3rd House

COMMUNICATION

RULED BY GEMINI

This house is about communication
and mental attitude, primarily how
you express yourself. It's also about
how you function within your family,
and how you travel to school or
work, and includes how you think,
speak, write and learn.

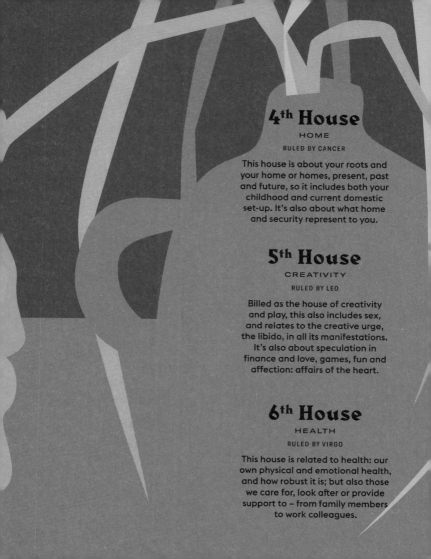

4th House
HOME
RULED BY CANCER

This house is about your roots and your home or homes, present, past and future, so it includes both your childhood and current domestic set-up. It's also about what home and security represent to you.

5th House
CREATIVITY
RULED BY LEO

Billed as the house of creativity and play, this also includes sex, and relates to the creative urge, the libido, in all its manifestations. It's also about speculation in finance and love, games, fun and affection: affairs of the heart.

6th House
HEALTH
RULED BY VIRGO

This house is related to health: our own physical and emotional health, and how robust it is; but also those we care for, look after or provide support to – from family members to work colleagues.

7th **House**

PARTNERSHIPS

RULED BY LIBRA

The opposite of the first house, this reflects shared goals and intimate partnerships, our choice of life partner and how successful our relationships might be. It also reflects partnerships and adversaries in our professional world.

8th **House**

REGENERATION

RULED BY SCORPIO

For death, read regeneration or spiritual transformation: this house also reflects legacies and what you inherit after death, in personality traits or materially. And because regeneration requires sex, it's also about sex and sexual emotions.

9th **House**

TRAVEL

RULED BY SAGITTARIUS

The house of long-distance travel and exploration, this is also about the broadening of the mind that travel can bring, and how that might express itself. It also reflects the sending out of ideas, which can come about from literary effort or publication.

11ᵗʰ House

FRIENDSHIPS

RULED BY AQUARIUS

The eleventh house is
about friendship groups and
acquaintances, vision and ideas,
and is less about immediate
gratification but more concerning
longer-term dreams and how these
might be realised through our ability
to work harmoniously with others.

12ᵗʰ House

SECRETS

RULED BY PISCES

Considered the most spiritual
house, it is also the house of the
unconscious, of secrets and of what
might lie hidden, the metaphorical
skeleton in the closet. It also reflects
the secret ways we might self-
sabotage or imprison our own
efforts by not exploring them.

10ᵗʰ House

ASPIRATIONS

RULED BY CAPRICORN

This represents our aspiration and
status, how we'd like to be elevated
in public standing (or not), our
ambitions, image and what we'd
like to attain in life, through
our own efforts.

The ascendant

Otherwise known as your rising sign, this is the sign of the zodiac that appears at the horizon as dawn breaks on the day of your birth, depending on your location in the world and time of birth. This is why knowing your time of birth is a useful factor in astrology, because your 'rising sign' yields a lot of information about those aspects of your character that are more on show, how you present yourself and how you are seen by others. So, even if you are a Sun Libra, but have Cancer rising, you may be seen as someone who is maternal, with a noticeable commitment to the domestic life in one way or another. Knowing your own ascendant – or that of another person – will often help explain why there doesn't seem to be such a direct correlation between their personality and their Sun sign.

As long as you know your time of birth and where you were born, working out your ascendant using an online tool or app is very easy (see page 108). Just ask your mum or other family members, or check your birth certificate (in those countries that include a birth time). If the astrological chart were a clock face, the ascendant would be at the 9 o'clock position.

The descendant

The descendant gives an indication of a possible life partner, based on the idea that opposites attract. Once you know your ascendant, the descendant is easy to work out as it is always six signs away: for example, if your ascendant is Virgo, your descendant is Pisces. If the astrological chart were a clock face, the descendant would be at the 3 o'clock position.

The midheaven (MC)

Also included in the birth chart is the position of the midheaven or MC (from the Latin, *medium coeli*, meaning middle of the heavens), which indicates your attitude towards your work, career and professional standing. If the astrological chart were a clock face, the MC would be at the 12 o'clock position.

The IC

Finally, your IC (from the Latin, *imum coeli*, meaning the lowest part of the heavens) indicates your attitude towards your home and family, and is also related to the end of your life. Your IC will be directly opposite your MC: for example, if your MC is Aquarius, your IC is Leo. If the astrological chart were a clock face, the IC would be at the 6 o'clock position.

Saturn return

Saturn is one of the slower-moving planets, taking around 28 years to complete its orbit around the Sun and return to the place it occupied at the time of your birth. This return can last between two to three years and be very noticeable in the period coming up to our thirtieth and sixtieth birthdays, often considered to be significant 'milestone' birthdays.

Because the energy of Saturn is sometimes experienced as demanding, this isn't always an easy period of life. A wise teacher or a hard taskmaster, some consider the Saturn effect as 'cruel to be kind' in the way that many good teachers can be, keeping us on track like a rigorous personal trainer.

Everyone experiences their Saturn return relevant to their circumstances, but it is a good time to take stock, let go of the stuff in your life that no longer serves you and revise your expectations, while being unapologetic about what you would like to include more of in your life. So if you are experiencing or anticipating this life event, embrace and work with it because what you learn now – about yourself, mainly – is worth knowing, however turbulent it might be, and can pay dividends in how you manage the next 28 years!

Mercury retrograde

Even those with little interest in astrology often take notice when the planet Mercury is retrograde. Astrologically, retrogrades are periods when planets are stationary but, as we continue to move forwards, Mercury 'appears' to move backwards. There is a shadow period either side of a retrograde period, when it could be said to be slowing down or speeding up, which can also be a little turbulent. Generally speaking, the advice is not to make any important moves related to communication on a retrograde and, even if a decision is made, know that it's likely to change.

Given that Mercury is the planet of communication, you can immediately see why there are concerns about its retrograde status and its link to communication failures – of the old-fashioned sort when the post office loses a letter, or the more modern technological variety when your computer crashes

– causing problems. Mercury retrograde can also affect travel, with delays in flights or train times, traffic jams or collisions. Mercury also influences personal communications: listening, speaking, being heard (or not), and can cause confusion or arguments. It can also affect more formal agreements, like contracts between buyer and seller.

These retrograde periods occur three to four times a year, lasting for roughly three weeks, with a shadow period either side. The dates in which it happens also mean it occurs within a specific astrological sign. If, for example, it occurs between 25 October and 15 November, its effect would be linked to the characteristics of Scorpio. In addition, those Sun sign Scorpios, or those with Scorpio in significant placements in their chart, may also experience a greater effect.

Mercury retrograde dates are easy to find from an astrological table, or ephemeris, and online. These can be used in order to avoid planning events that might be affected around these times. How Mercury retrograde may affect you more personally requires knowledge of your birth chart and an understanding of its more specific combination of influences with the signs and planets in your chart.

If you are going to weather a Mercury retrograde more easily, be aware that glitches can occur so, to some extent, expect delays and double-check details. Stay positive if postponements occur and consider this period an opportunity to slow down, review or reconsider ideas in your business or your personal life. Use the time to correct mistakes or reshape plans, preparing for when any stuck energy can shift and you can move forward again more smoothly.

Further reading

Astrology Decoded (2013)
by Sue Merlyn Farebrother;
published by Rider

Astrology for Dummies
(2007) by Rae Orion;
published by Wiley Publishing

*Chart Interpretation
Handbook: Guidelines for
Understanding the Essentials
of the Birth Chart* (1990)
by Stephen Arroyo;
published by CRCS
Publications

Jung's Studies in Astrology
(2018) by Liz Greene;
published by RKP

*The Only Astrology
Book You'll Ever Need*
(2012) by Joanne Woolfolk;
published by Taylor Trade

Websites

astro.com

astrologyzone.com

jessicaadams.com

shelleyvonstrunkel.com

Apps

Astrostyle

Co-Star

Susan Miller's Astrology Zone

The Daily Horoscope

The Pattern

Time Passages

Acknowledgements

Particular thanks are due to my trusty
team of Taureans. Firstly, to Kate Pollard,
Publishing Director at Hardie Grant, for her
passion for beautiful books and for commissioning
this series. And to Bex Fitzsimons for all her good
natured and conscientious editing. And finally to
Evi O. Studio, whose illustration and design talents
have produced small works of art. With such a
star-studded team, these books can only
shine and for that, my thanks.

About the author

Stella Andromeda has been studying astrology for over 30 years, believing that a knowledge of the constellations of the skies and their potential for psychological interpretation can be a useful tool. This extension of her study into book form makes modern insights about the ancient wisdom of the stars easily accessible, sharing her passion that reflection and self-knowledge only empowers us in life. With her sun in Taurus, Aquarius ascendant and Moon in Cancer, she utilises earth, air and water to inspire her own astrological journey.

Published in 2019 by Hardie Grant Books,
an imprint of Hardie Grant Publishing

Hardie Grant Books (London)
5th & 6th Floors
52–54 Southwark Street
London SE1 1UN

Hardie Grant Books (Melbourne)
Building 1, 658 Church Street
Richmond, Victoria 3121

hardiegrantbooks.com

All rights reserved. No part of this publication may be reproduced,
stored in a retrieval system or transmitted in any form by any
means, electronic, mechanical, photocopying, recording or
otherwise, without the prior written permission of
the publishers and copyright holders.

The moral rights of the author have been asserted.

Copyright text © Stella Andromeda
Copyright illustrations © Evi O. Studio

British Library Cataloguing-in-Publication Data. A catalogue record
for this book is available from the British Library.

Libra
ISBN: 9781784882709

10 9 8 7 6 5 4

Publishing Director: Kate Pollard
Junior Editor: Bex Fitzsimons
Art Direction and Illustrations: Evi O. Studio
Editor: Wendy Hobson
Production Controller: Sinead Hering
Colour reproduction by p2d
Printed and bound in China by Leo Paper Products Ltd.